SCIENTISTS

Are Saving the WORLD!

So WHO IS WORKING ON TIME TRAVEL?

Written by
SASKIA GWINN

Illustrated by
ANA ALBERO

MAGIC CAT PUBLISHING

NEW YORK

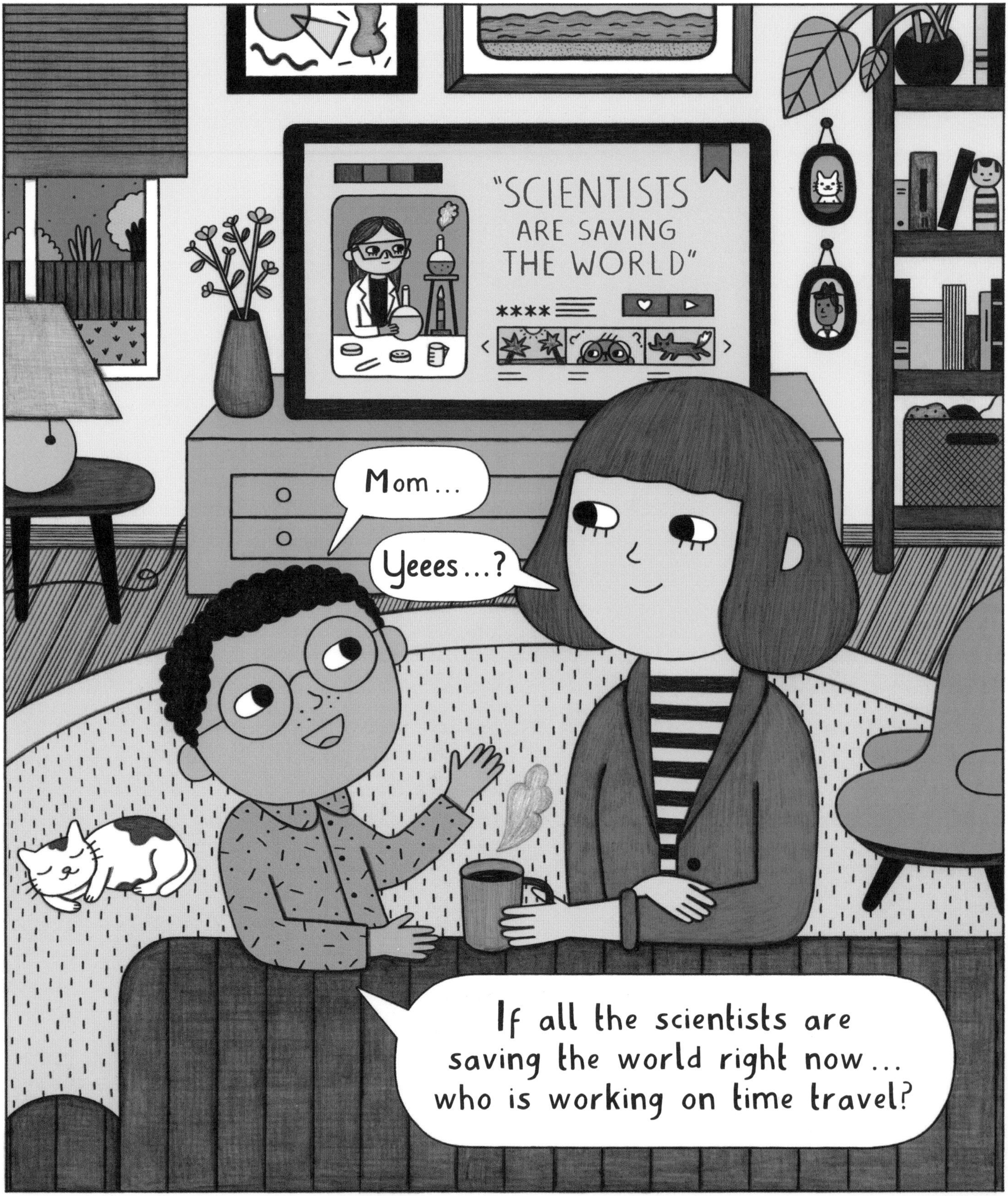
"SCIENTISTS ARE SAVING THE WORLD"
Mom...
Yeees...?
If all the scientists are saving the world right now... who is working on time travel?

Lots of other AMAZING scientists, of course! Scientists are out there doing terrific things all across the planet...

floating through space,

digging up dinosaurs...

and EVEN figuring out how to travel through time.

They're looking for rainbows,

eavesdropping on elephants,

To bring back a dinosaur?

You see, it's like this...

SCIENTISTS ARE DIGGING UP DINOSAURS

Scientists who dig up dinosaurs are called PALEONTOLOGISTS. They look for dinosaurs and ancient beasts everywhere ...

MARY ANNING dug up an ancient fossil with her brother when she was just twelve years old!

THIS IS AN ICHTHYOSAUR, NOT A CROC!

Mary inspired paleontologists to look for dinosaurs all over the world in ...

glaciers,   mountains,

Scientists take the things they find to museums. LOUIS R. PURNELL studied and identified fossils in a museum.

and rocks!

When they think they've found a dinosaur, they start digging, scooping, and drilling through stone.

BANG,

CRACK,

and **LOOK!**

They've found the bones of a BEAST.

Now we can see what a dinosaur skeleton looked like!

STEGOSAURUS

But can they travel back in time to get one?

I'm getting to that!

⟨ SCIENTISTS ARE ZOOMING THROUGH SPACE ⟩

Scientists who zoom through space are called ASTRONAUTS.
Different countries can have different names for space explorers.

LEONID KADENYUK was the first Ukrainian citizen to
BLAST OFF into space.

Astronauts WHOOSH into space to ...

build things,

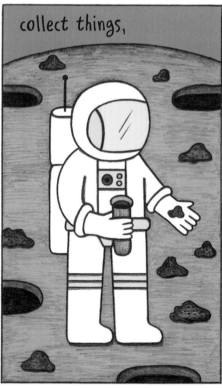

collect things,

grow things,

and help other astronauts.

LIU YANG of China has flown to space to test if it's safe for other astronauts to live there.

I'M A TAIKONAUT

Once space explorers complete their missions, they...

SHAKE,

SOAR,

and **SPLASH** back to Earth to tell other astronauts what space is like.

It takes thousands of scientists to launch a rocket!

x1000

Do scientists find out about the weather?

They do!

SCIENTISTS ARE FINDING RAINBOWS

Scientists who look out for amazing things like rainbows—and the Northern Lights!—are called METEOROLOGISTS.

Meteorologists love the weather. So they look for rainbows,

snowflakes,

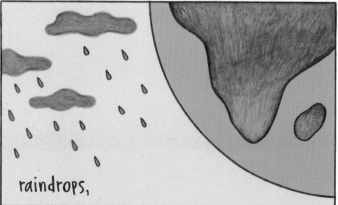

raindrops,

and storm clouds.

JOANNE SIMPSON found out why hot tower clouds create and drive hurricanes. Now we can tell when one is on its way.

LOOK OUT!

Meteorologists can also find out what clouds weigh!

about 100 elephants

1 cloud

Once METEOROLOGISTS predict what the weather will be like, they tell everyone. JUNE BACON-BERCEY told us when there would be SIZZLING sunshine.

Do scientists look for animals too?

YES! And they listen to them ...

SCIENTISTS ARE EAVESDROPPING ON ELEPHANTS

Scientists who listen to animals are called ACOUSTIC BIOLOGISTS. It's their job to hear the HULLABALOO of creatures in every corner of the world...

by sailing down rivers,

climbing tall trees,

and camping in RAIN FORESTS!

DEEPAL WARAKAGODA was rambling through the forest when heard something strange...

WHOO-OH

It was an owl that no one had ever heard before!

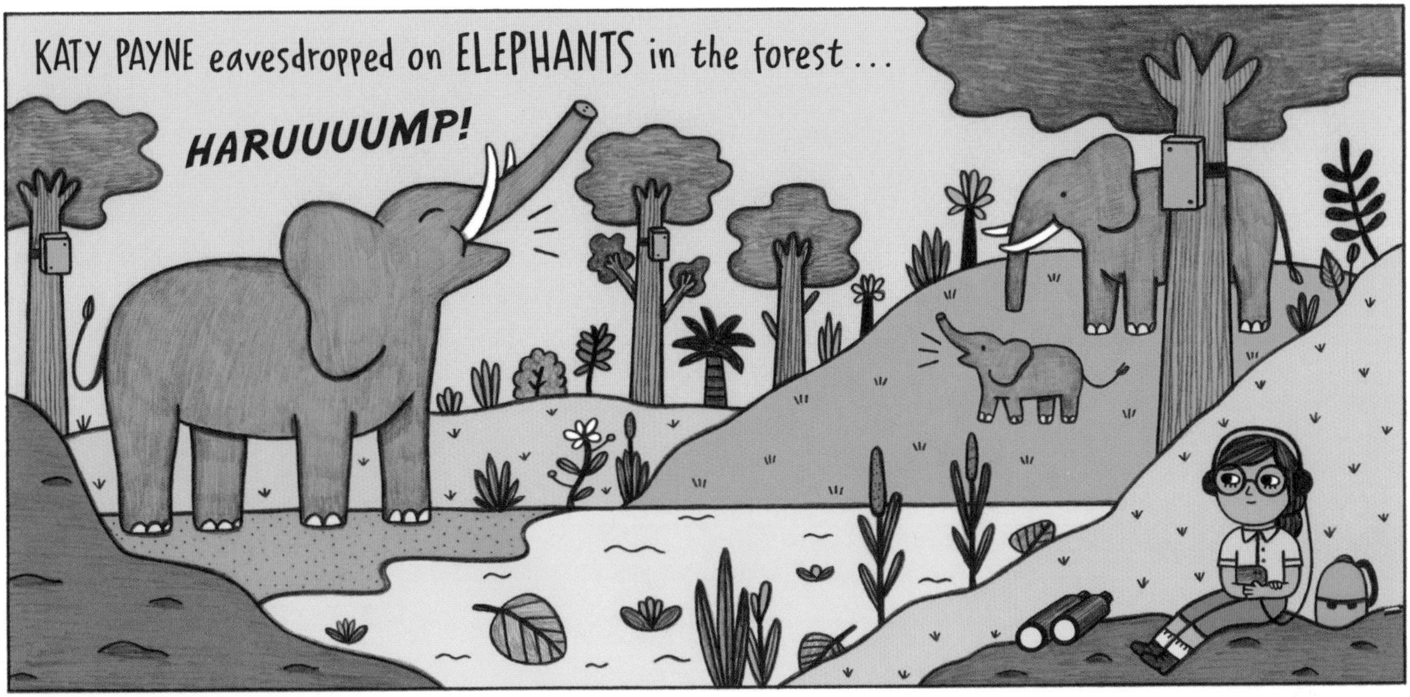
KATY PAYNE eavesdropped on ELEPHANTS in the forest . . .
HARUUUUMP!

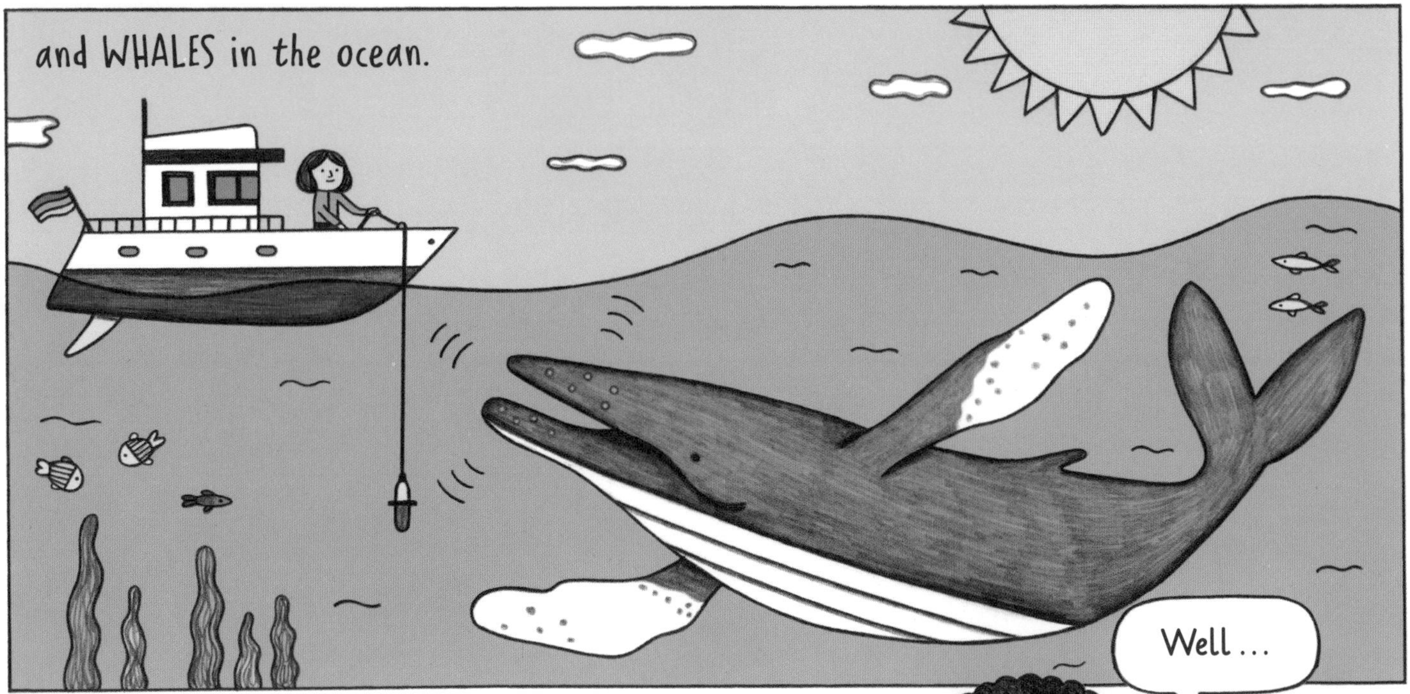
and WHALES in the ocean.

ACOUSTIC BIOLOGISTS record the sounds they hear and share them with important libraries.

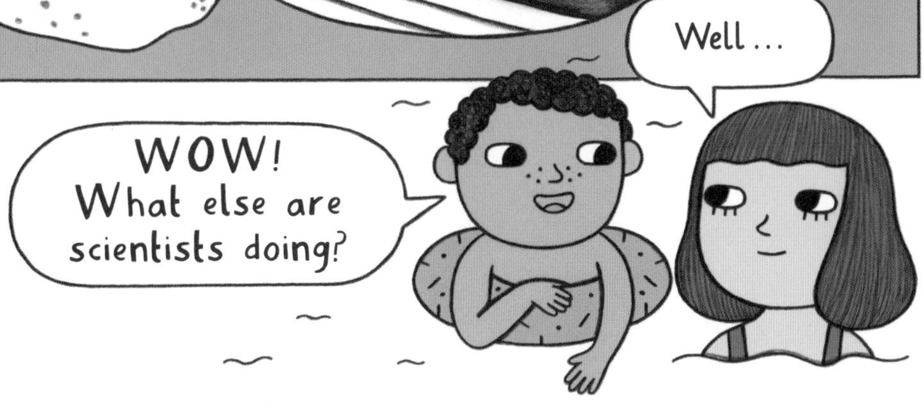
WOW! What else are scientists doing?
Well . . .

SCIENTISTS ARE BUILDING ROBOTS

Scientists who build robots are called ROBOTIC ENGINEERS. They build and operate robots for exciting places such as ...

movie sets,

farms,

and outer space! STEPHANIE WILSON is an engineer who operates robotic arms in space.

She helped astronauts carry out a MONUMENTAL space walk.

Engineers sometimes look at animals for inspiration to build robots that . . .

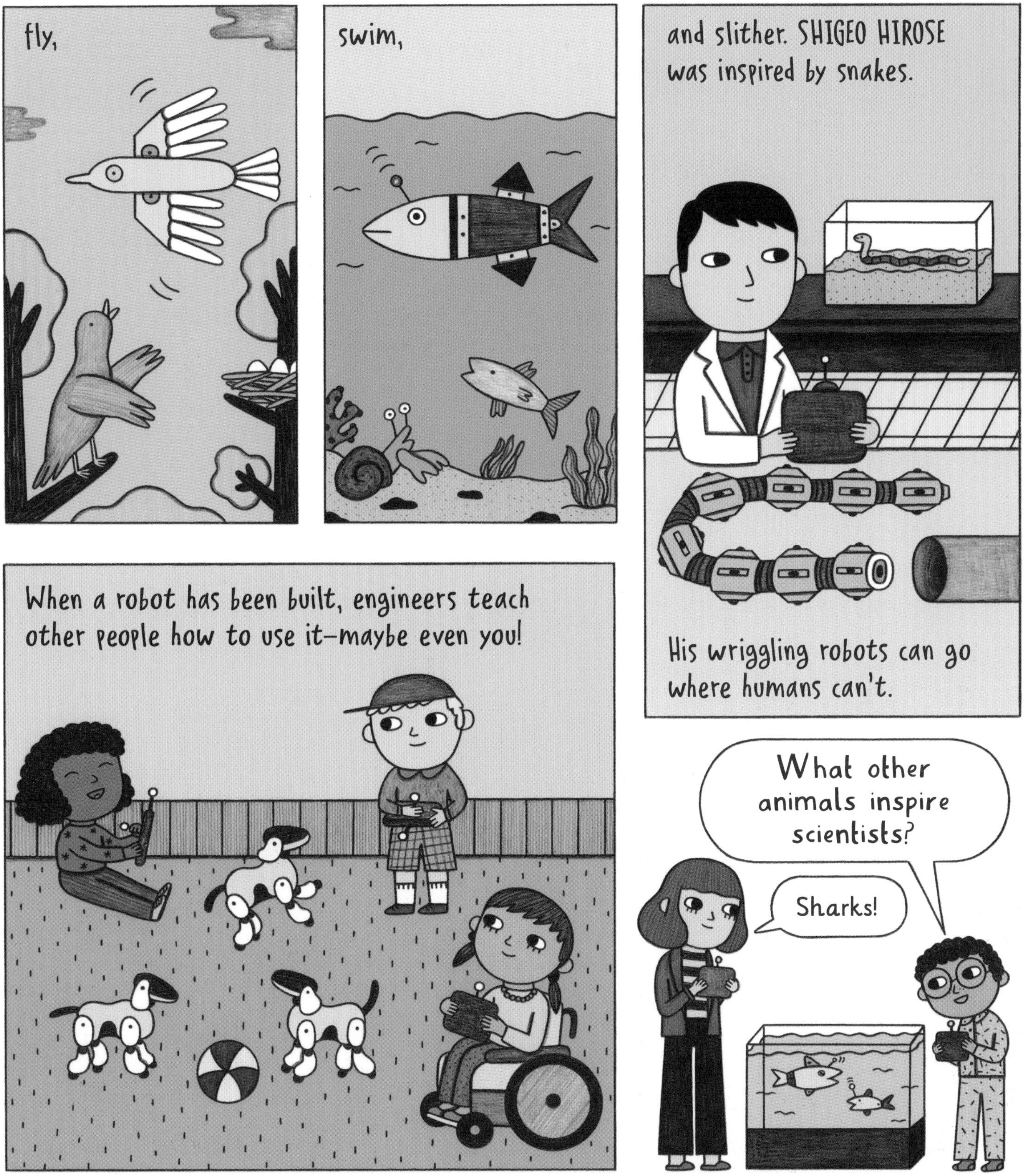
fly,
swim,
and slither. SHIGEO HIROSE was inspired by snakes.
His wriggling robots can go where humans can't.
When a robot has been built, engineers teach other people how to use it—maybe even you!
What other animals inspire scientists?
Sharks!

SCIENTISTS ARE SWIMMING WITH SHARKS

Scientists who swim with sharks are called MARINE BIOLOGISTS. They protect our oceans with their EPIC underwater adventures!

They sail,

dive,

and swim with fish...

stingrays...

and sharks!

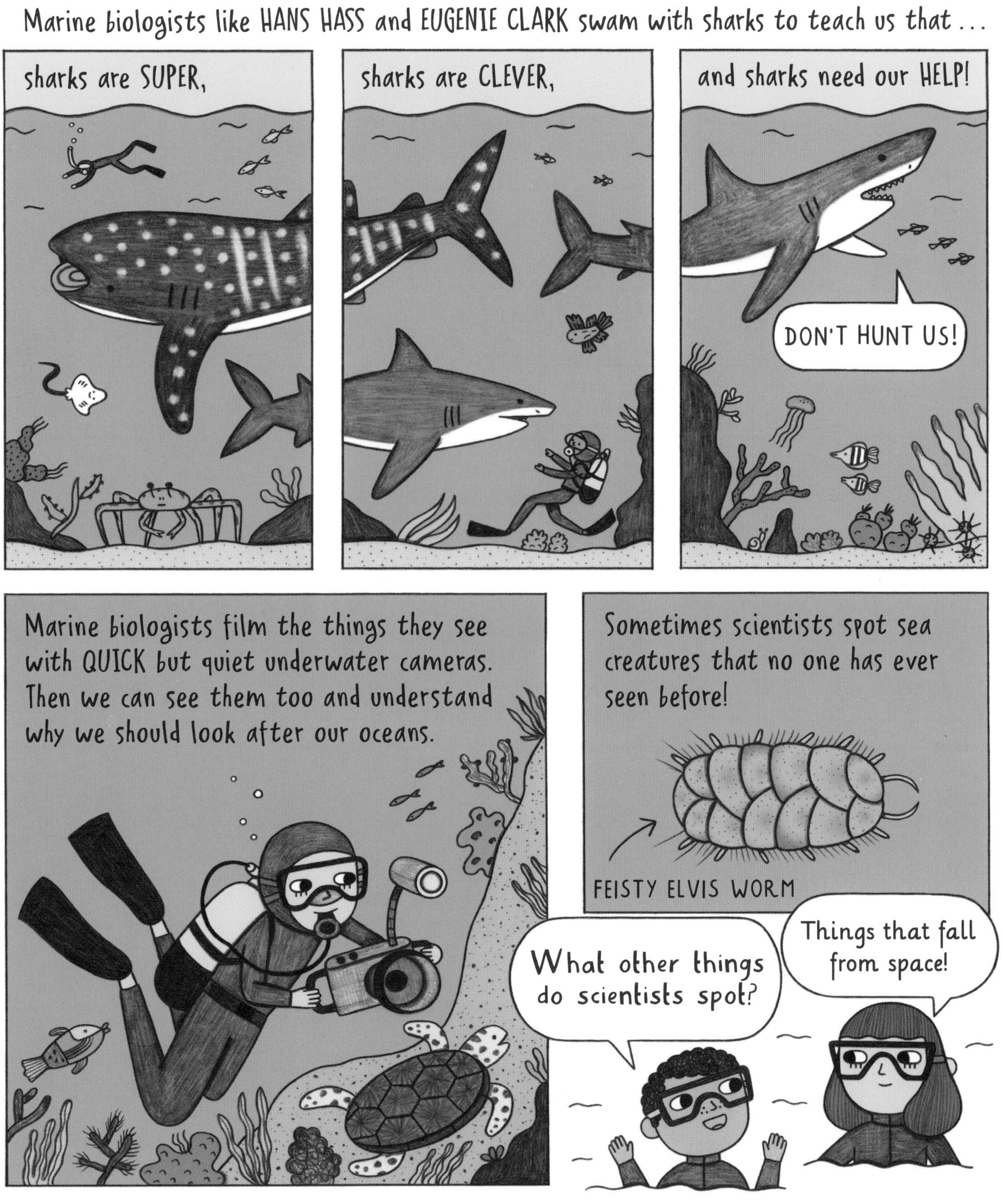
Marine biologists like HANS HASS and EUGENIE CLARK swam with sharks to teach us that . . .
sharks are SUPER,
sharks are CLEVER,
and sharks need our HELP!
DON'T HUNT US!
Marine biologists film the things they see with QUICK but quiet underwater cameras. Then we can see them too and understand why we should look after our oceans.
Sometimes scientists spot sea creatures that no one has ever seen before!
FEISTY ELVIS WORM
What other things do scientists spot?
Things that fall from space!

SCIENTISTS ARE COLLECTING ROCKS

Scientists who collect rocks are called GEOLOGISTS and they have the coolest rock collections EVER ...

NATALIE STARKEY is a geologist who finds rocks that have fallen from space.

Rocks such as ...

palm-sized pebbles ...

or meteorites, packed with gold.

Geologists send robots into space to pick up rocks too!

And sometimes, pieces of dying stars hitch a ride to Earth on meteors.

Soon geologists will study asteroid samples collected in space.

Geologists examine volcanoes too ...

in space,

on islands,

and in the ocean.

HARALDUR SIGURÐSSON finds out why volcanoes erupt.

BUBBLE

RUMBLE

POP!

Rocks are Earth's treasures!

Yes. Earth is full of treasures ...

Geologists write down what volcanic rock is made of.

SCIENTISTS ARE STUDYING SEEDS

Scientists who study seeds and plants are called BOTANISTS and they study the plants of the world like the TREASURES they are.

Botanists help plants grow because our planet needs them.

Botanists figure out how to keep plants healthy.

Plants make oxygen . . . so botanists protect them.

LIGHT

OXYGEN

CARBON DIOXIDE

WATER

JANAKI AMMAL protected PRECIOUS plants and FABULOUS flowers that feed and shelter animals.

Janaki developed India's sugarcane crops and created NEW varieties that people could grow themselves.

Botanists write books about plants so that we can protect our planet-saving superheroes.

YNES MEXIA journeyed along the Amazon River by boat, raft, and canoe to collect plants most people had never seen before.

Do scientists protect bugs too?

They sure do...

SCIENTISTS ARE SPYING ON CENTIPEDES

Scientists who spy on centipedes and other many-legged BUGS are called ARTHROPODOLOGISTS...

FILIPPO SILVESTRI had a terrific time scoping out centipedes and marveling at millipedes.

Insects help planet-saving plants to keep Earth GREEN.

That's why scientists don't just spy on centipedes, they also...

BOGGLE at bees that help wild plants grow,

CARE about crickets,

CHIRP CHIRP

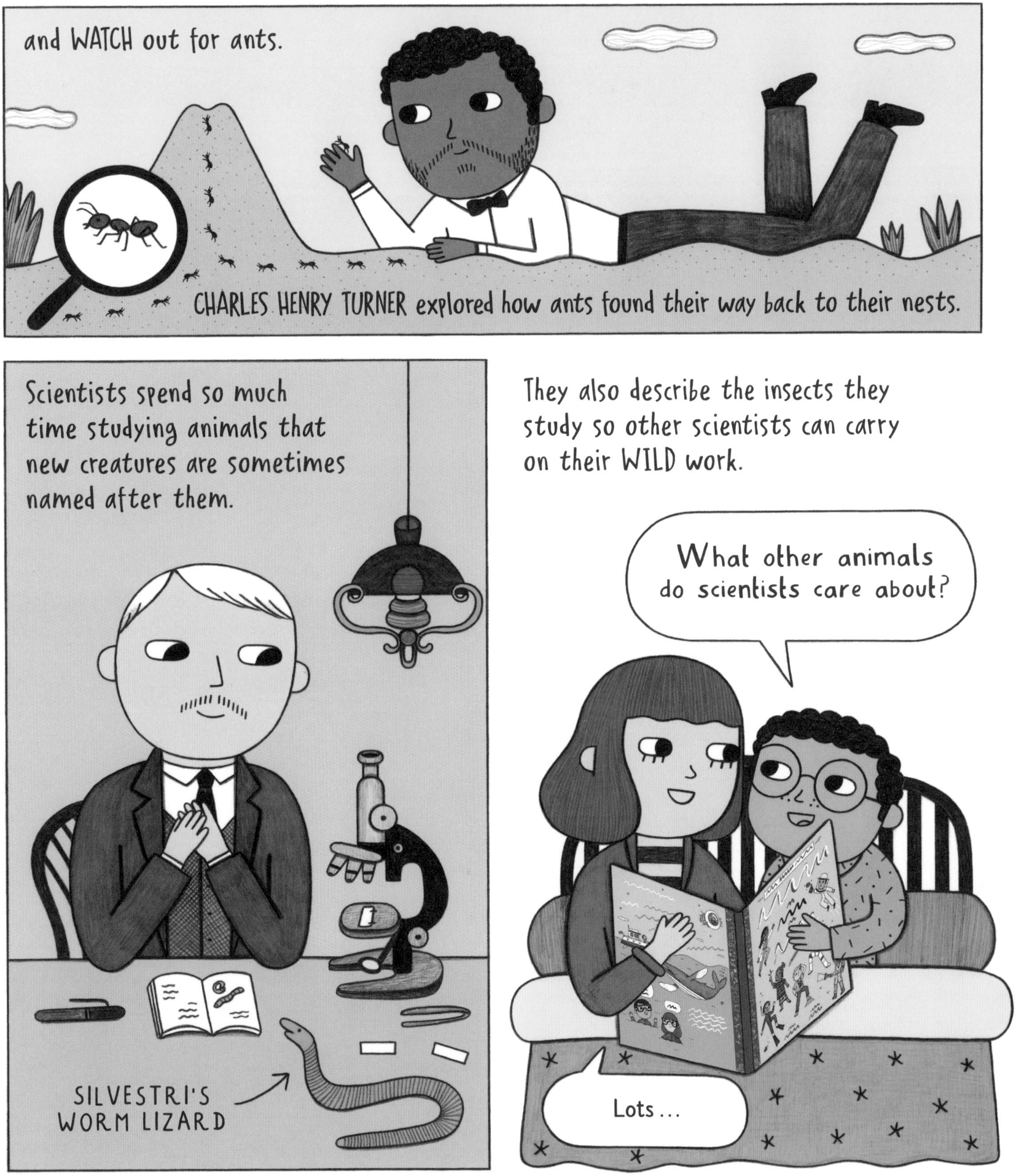
and WATCH out for ants.
CHARLES HENRY TURNER explored how ants found their way back to their nests.
Scientists spend so much time studying animals that new creatures are sometimes named after them.
SILVESTRI'S WORM LIZARD
They also describe the insects they study so other scientists can carry on their WILD work.
What other animals do scientists care about?
Lots...

SCIENTISTS ARE PROTECTING OUR PLANET

Conservationists, zoologists, climatologists, and many scientists you've read about in this book study Earth in order to work out how to protect it. Animals are in danger because our planet is getting warmer. This is called climate change.

NARWHAL

MY ICE IS MELTING!

REINDEER

IT'S HARD TO FIND FOOD!

LEMMING

SNOW USED TO HIDE US!

Scientists discovered that we can help protect our planet against climate change by ...

burning less fuel,

wasting less food,

and planting more trees.

WANGARI MAATHAI helped to plant 50 million trees.

SIR DAVID ATTENBOROUGH has moved us to combat climate change with his AWESOME nature shows.

Scientists work tirelessly to tell us how we can save our world.

SCIENTISTS ARE SAVING LIVES

Scientists are saving people's lives with MARVELOUS medicines. There are too many types of lifesaving scientists to list here but...

You may have heard of the ones who invent vaccines.

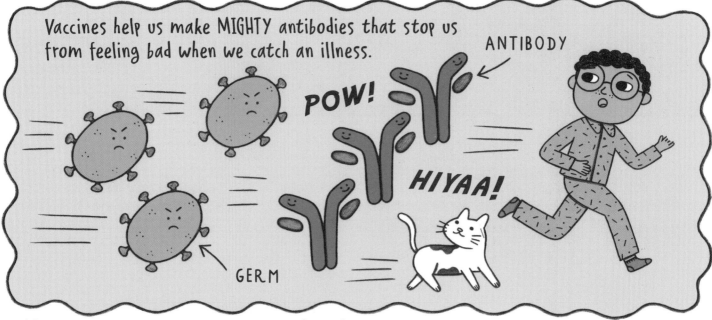

Vaccines help us make MIGHTY antibodies that stop us from feeling bad when we catch an illness.

ANTIBODY

POW!

HIYAA!

GERM

Many years ago, RACHEL SCHNEERSON helped invent a vaccine that has since saved millions of lives.

HAEMOPHILUS INFLUENZAE TYPE B

Sometimes lifesaving scientists have to work SUPER fast...

UĞUR ŞAHIN and ÖZLEM TÜRECI are two of the scientists behind the Pfizer-BioNTech vaccine protecting us against COVID-19.

By looking after all living things, scientists are saving the wonderful world we know.

SCIENTISTS ARE STUDYING THE SPEED OF LIGHT

Scientists who work out how light travels through space are called ASTROPHYSICISTS. They study the most EXOTIC thing in the entire UNIVERSE . . .

SUPERMASSIVE, hyperactive black holes called BLAZARS!

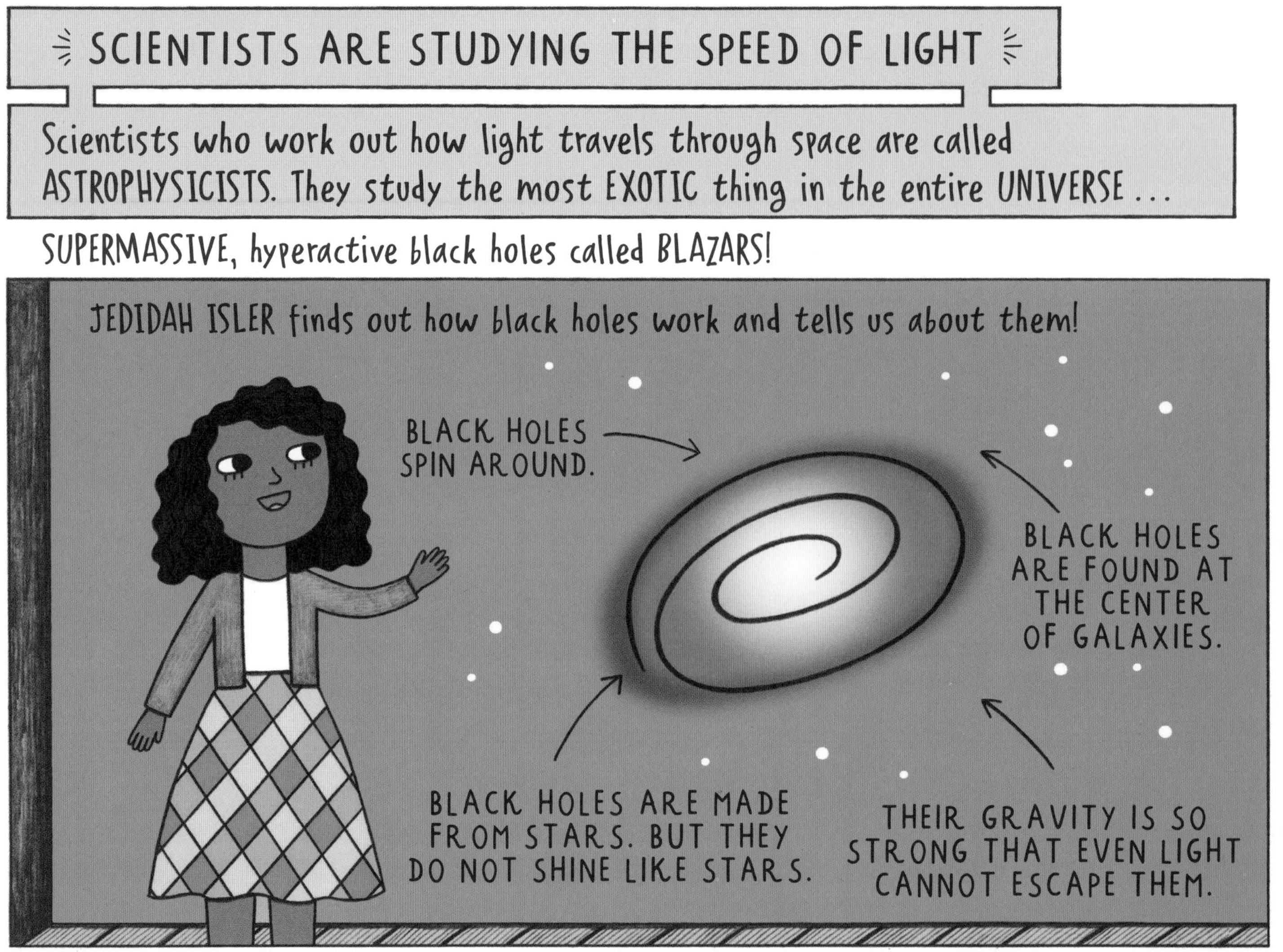
JEDIDAH ISLER finds out how black holes work and tells us about them!
BLACK HOLES SPIN AROUND.
BLACK HOLES ARE FOUND AT THE CENTER OF GALAXIES.
BLACK HOLES ARE MADE FROM STARS. BUT THEY DO NOT SHINE LIKE STARS.
THEIR GRAVITY IS SO STRONG THAT EVEN LIGHT CANNOT ESCAPE THEM.

ASTROPHYSICISTS also study the size and shape of space.

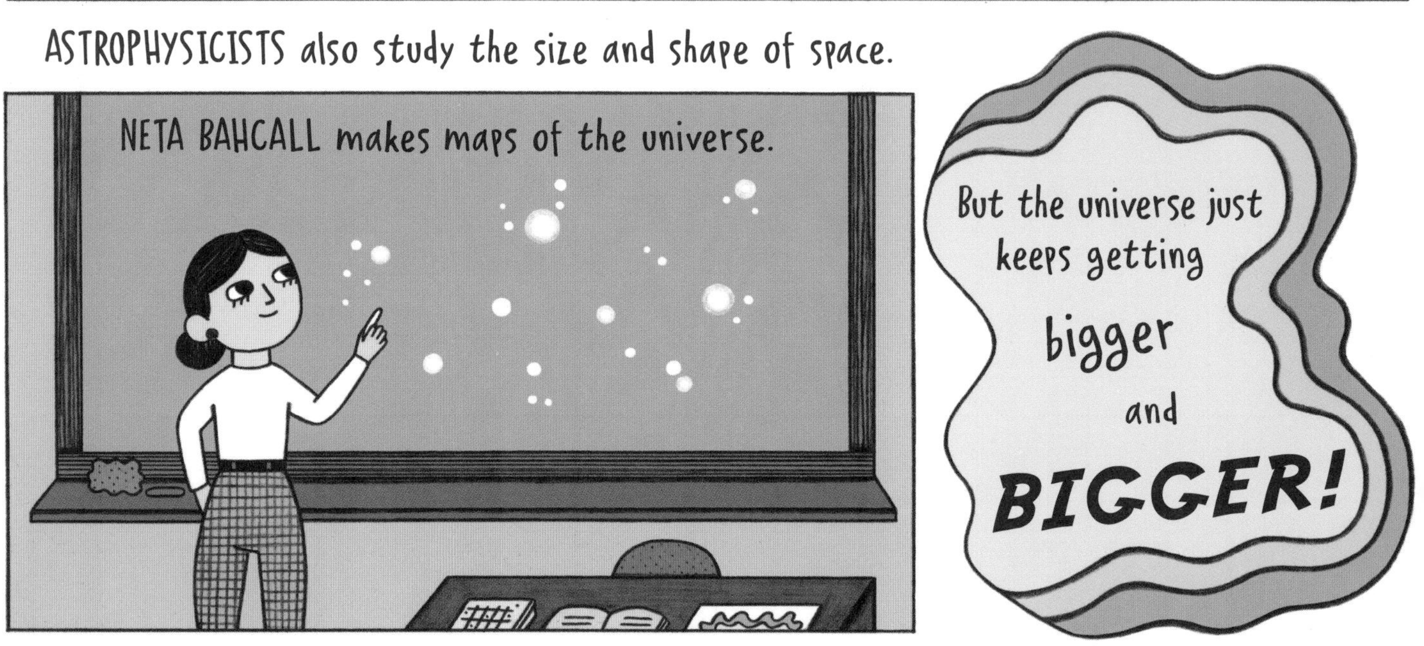
NETA BAHCALL makes maps of the universe.

But the universe just keeps getting bigger and **BIGGER!**

Scientists investigate fast how things travel through space too...

SOME scientists wonder if we can travel through space faster than the speed of light.

People call it TIME TRAVEL.

Maybe one day scientists will figure out how to travel to every corner of the universe and even ... back through time.

Scientists like ME?

That's right! Because...

So now you see, all kinds of scientists are out there doing spectacularly SUPER things. They started off ...

asking questions about dinosaurs,

staring at stars,

wondering about whales,

watching things grow,

and dreaming of adventure just like...

YOU!

That's how grown-up scientists begin. They were once little scientists too!

WHICH SCIENTIST INSPIRES YOU?

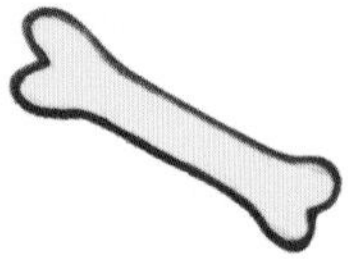

PALEONTOLOGISTS

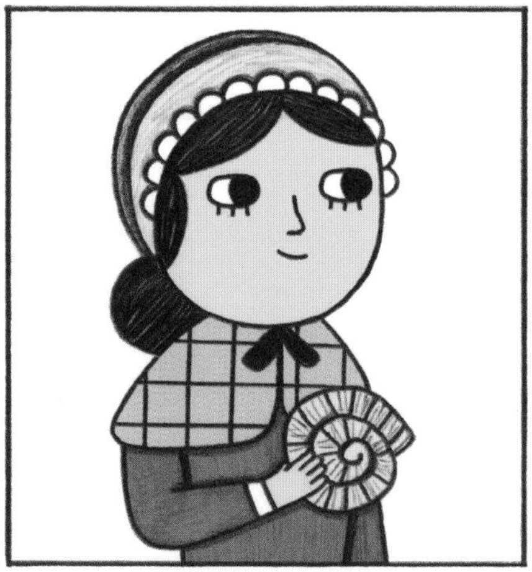

MARY ANNING

Born 1799 • Died 1847

Mary Anning was a paleontologist who dug up prehistoric beasts. Mary's dad taught her how to look for fossils when she was only five. When they found a fossil, they would clean it up and sometimes sell it in their shop. Mary and her brother dug up an ichthyosaur when Mary was just twelve years old. At first, scientists thought it was a crocodile! Mary has inspired other paleontologists around the world to find dinosaurs and other ancient animals. Paleontologists are still digging for fossils along the English coastline, where Mary made her discoveries. In fact, so many fossils have been found there that it is now called the "Jurassic Coast."

ASTRONAUTS

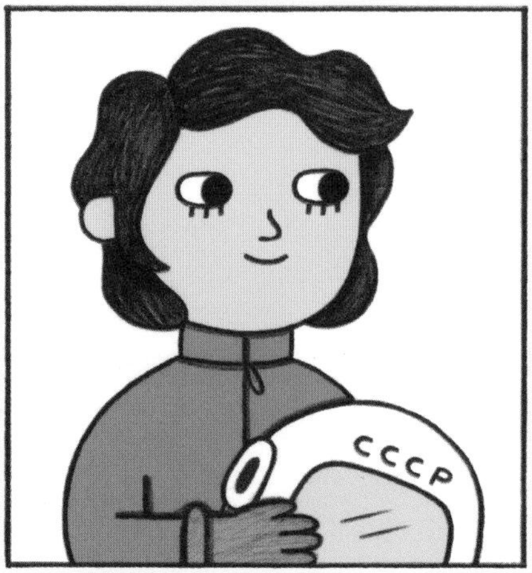
CCCP

LEONID KADENYUK

Born 1951 • Died 2018

Leonid made history when he became the first Ukrainian citizen to zoom into space onboard the U.S. space shuttle *Columbia*. During his mega mission, Leonid orbited Earth 252 times, traveling 6.5 million miles in just over 15.5 days. He trained as a botanist too so he could carry out biology experiments in space to see how plants grow in microgravity. He also observed the effect that weightlessness has on plant biomass (a mix of important elements found in plants including carbon). Another of Leonid's jobs in space was to study the atmospheric layers of the sun!

METEOROLOGISTS

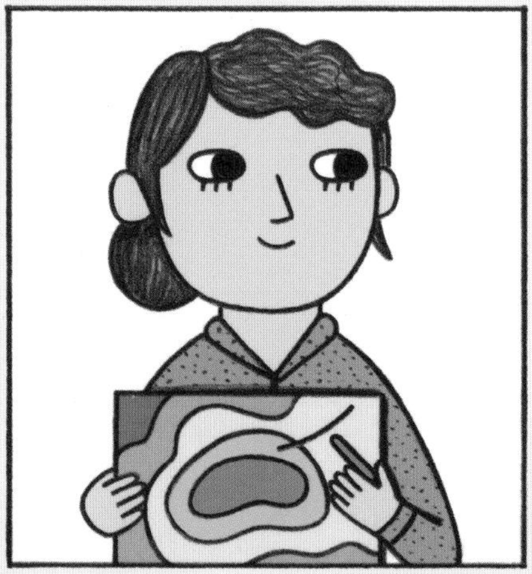

JOANNE SIMPSON

Born 1923 • Died 2010

Joanne was an award-winning meteorologist. Joanne started her career as a student pilot, which led her to study meteorology. Later, along with another scientist, Herbert Riehl, she explained that tall tropical clouds pump out heat to create powerful, whipping winds. Joanne also developed the first computer cloud model and worked for NASA, where she helped with a special mission to measure tropical rainfall from space—a mission that is still running today. Joanne drew detailed maps of cloud formations too. She was the first woman ever to receive the International Meteorological Organization Prize.

LOUIS R. PURNELL
Born 1920 · Died 2001

Louis was one of the Tuskegee Airmen who flew planes in the World War II. When the war finished, he worked at the Smithsonian National Museum of Natural History. He traveled the world identifying ancient fossils and samples from the bottom of the ocean and wrote down important information about nautiloids and cephalopods. (Nautiloids are ancient sea creatures with shells and tentacles. Cephalopods exist today—without shells—as octopuses, squid, and cuttlefish.) His catalog of nautiloids and cephalopods is still used by scientists. Louis also worked at the Smithsonian National Air and Space Museum, where he became an expert on the history of spacecraft and spacesuits.

LIU YANG
Born 1978

Yang was the first Chinese woman to fly into space. Before she trained as an astronaut, Yang used to fly planes in the army. After completing a challenging two-year astronaut program, and it wasn't long before she was given an incredible cosmic mission! Yang and two other astronauts lifted off from the edge of the Gobi Desert in the Shenzhou 9 spacecraft, and from there they flew to a space module. In space, Yang carried out special assignments and was in charge of all medical experiments. Fitness is important for space explorers and Yang even performed tai chi, a martial art, in space.

JUNE BACON-BERCEY
Born 1928 · Died 2019

June Bacon-Bercey was a trailblazing meteorologist who often appeared on television. June was curious about science from an early age and became the first Black woman to obtain a degree in meteorology. Her spectacular knowledge of Earth's atmosphere won her a weather reporting job on television. She used her clever calculations to successfully predict when hot, stormy, or cold weather was coming. June won awards for her amazing on-air meteorology and weather predictions. She also created a scholarship program to support women studying science. She taught children in schools about math and science too, inspiring them to follow their dreams like she did.

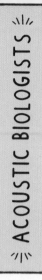

ACOUSTIC BIOLOGISTS

DEEPAL WARAKAGODA
Born 1965

Deepal is an ornithologist (bird scientist) and expert in bird sounds. One day, Deepal was trekking through the depths of the Sinharaja Forest Reserve in Sri Lanka. There among the racket of animal sounds, Deepal heard an unusual noise no one had recorded before! Deepal spent six years revisiting the forest to search for its owner until, on one dark night, the beam of his flashlight finally shone on a little owl hiding in the trees. It was identified as a Serendib Scops Owl, a rare night owl and the first new bird to be found on the island since 1868! Deepal has spent years studying and writing books about birds to find out and share more about them.

ROBOTIC ENGINEERS

STEPHANIE WILSON
Born 1966

Stephanie grew up looking at the night sky, wondering what might be out there. Now she is an award-winning astronaut and aerospace engineer who helped make important equipment for space missions! She's flown to the International Space Station three times and spent more than forty-two days in space. She helped transfer supplies and equipment to the space station and has worked as a flight engineer. On one cosmic trip, she served as the robotic arm operator during a space walk. Back on the ground, she helped two other astronauts carry out a space walk by talking to them and issuing instructions from mission control while they were working on important repairs.

MARINE BIOLOGISTS

HANS HASS
Born 1919 · Died 2013

Hans Hass was a marine biologist, diver, filmmaker, photographer, and underwater explorer who loved to dive with sharks. Hans swam with thousands of sharks to tell the world how amazing sharks were at a time when they were feared by many. Hans also took photos of mind-blowing coral reefs, spectacular stingrays, and awe-inspiring octopuses as well as many other types of fish and ocean-dwelling creatures. Hans made films and wrote dozens of books to tell us about Earth's amazing underwater world and his own ocean adventures. It's said that Hans helped to develop an underwater camera too!

KATY PAYNE
Born 1937

Katharine (Katy) is an acoustic biologist who became known for recording the sounds of elephants and whales. Katy realized she might have made a new discovery when she heard elephants communicating with one another at a zoo in Oregon, USA. Returning to the zoo with special recording equipment, Katy recorded elephants to find out that they were communicating using sounds below the range of human hearing. Katy is cofounder of the Elephant Listening Project, an organization that helps to preserve the tropical forests of Africa. Katy and her husband, Roger, recorded whale songs too. While out on the ocean, they made the awe-inspiring discovery that humpback whales sing songs. Katy and Roger's important work helps us understand and protect animals.

SHIGEO HIROSE
Born 1947

Shigeo specializes in mechanical and control engineering to help him make remarkable robots. He watched how real snakes could move, bend, and lift their bodies, or climb up trees and swim through water. Then Shigeo set to work with other scientists and students to build a snakelike robot with an important mission in mind. Shigeo's robots are designed to explore places on Earth that humans can't easily get to—places such as underwater caves or underground pipes. It is hoped that they will be able to help with disaster rescue missions one day. Shigeo was inspired by insects too. After spotting a daddy longlegs wandering up the stairs, he designed a robot with legs.

EUGENIE CLARK
Born 1922 · Died 2015

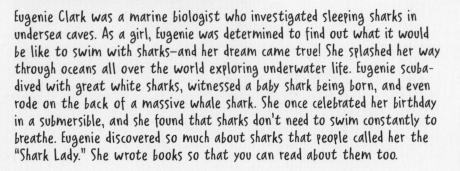

Eugenie Clark was a marine biologist who investigated sleeping sharks in undersea caves. As a girl, Eugenie was determined to find out what it would be like to swim with sharks—and her dream came true! She splashed her way through oceans all over the world exploring underwater life. Eugenie scuba-dived with great white sharks, witnessed a baby shark being born, and even rode on the back of a massive whale shark. She once celebrated her birthday in a submersible, and she found that sharks don't need to swim constantly to breathe. Eugenie discovered so much about sharks that people called her the "Shark Lady." She wrote books so that you can read about them too.

⋛ NATALIE STARKEY ⋚
Born 1982

Natalie Starkey is a geologist and cosmochemist who opens up space rocks to find out what's in them. As a child, she loved to look at shooting stars in the sky. Now she looks at stardust that's fallen to Earth from space as well as rocks picked up by robots on space missions! Natalie studies comets and asteroids that tell us about our solar system millions of years ago. Studying space rocks even helps Natalie find out how our solar system was created. She writes cosmic books about stardust and space volcanoes. Natalie learns about volcanoes on Earth too, including ancient volcanoes in the Arctic and active volcanoes in Iceland and the Caribbean.

⋛ JANAKI AMMAL ⋚
Born 1897 · Died 1984

Janaki was a groundbreaking botanist who protected plant life in India. She also developed a species of sugarcane that Indian people could grow on their own land. Janaki stood up for Silent Valley National Park in Kerala, a forest that's home to thousands of plants, trees, and animals. Janaki joined the many activists who were against a power plant project in the area—a project that would have destroyed the valley. The protesters were successful, and the project was abandoned. Janaki did so much for plant life that there are even flowers named after her, including a famous rose with yellow petals and a magnolia with bright white petals and purple stamens.

⋛ FILIPPO SILVESTRI ⋚
Born 1873 · Died 1949

Filippo was an awe-inspiring arthropodologist and entomologist (insect scientist) who cataloged the differences between centipedes and millipedes. Filippo studied a special type of termite and marveled at animal species that give birth to identical young from a single egg cell. He studied their egg structures to find out how this happens as well as how many identical young one egg could produce. Filippo wowed the world so much with his bug knowledge that scientists named an insect after him called Silvestri's Worm Lizard, a type of long worm lizard that is native to South America.

HARALDUR SIGURÐSSON
Born 1939

Haraldur is a famous geologist and volcanologist who has visited volcanoes all over the world, from Africa to America and Indonesia to Italy. He even explores volcanoes in the ocean. Haraldur has helped reconstruct major volcanic explosions that happened a long, long time ago, including the eruption of Mount Vesuvius in Italy. Haraldur once helped other scientists find the lost kingdom of Tambora in Indonesia. The kingdom had been buried by a terrible volcanic explosion in 1815. Haraldur and a team of colleagues uncovered bowls, pots, and tools, among other artifacts, during their archaeological dig. Their findings help tell us about the lifestyles of the people who lived there.

YNES MEXIA
Born 1870 · Died 1938

Ynes loved tracking down types of plants she hadn't come across before, sometimes traveling up mighty mountains and rowing down swampy rivers. Ynes journeyed thousands of miles along the Amazon River, collecting plant specimens along the way. During the expedition, she traveled some of the way in a dugout canoe. At night, Ynes and her crew camped on sandy beaches. Ynes gathered over 145,000 different plant samples during her expeditions in South America and Alaska. During her life, Ynes discovered 500 new species of plants and some are even named after her, such as the *Mimosa mexiae*. You can see the plant specimens Ynes collected in museums today.

CHARLES HENRY TURNER
Born 1867 · Died 1923

Charles was a pioneering zoologist (animal scientist) and entomologist who found out interesting things about bugs. Charles set up nests for ants to find out how they found their way home. He discovered that ants find their way by learning about their surroundings and remembering them. Charles studied other bugs too, including wasps and moths. Most people back then thought that bees navigated the world using wind and sunlight, but he observed that bees use their memories to find their way home. Charles also found out that honeybees can see in color and recognize patterns. During his life, Charles led many studies to show that insects can learn and hear!

CONSERVATIONISTS

⇒ WANGARI MAATHAI ⇐
Born 1940 · Died 2011

Wangari grew up in a small village in Kenya, surrounded by beautiful forests that were home to leopards and elephants. Wangari saw that too many of Kenya's trees were being cut down, so she founded the Green Belt Movement, a campaign to help local women plant more trees. The Green Belt Movement grew and grew until hundreds of groups were planting thousands of trees. Now, well over 50 million trees have been planted and the movement has spread across dozens of countries. Planting trees creates important habitats for animals and is also a way to help combat climate change. Wangari was the first African woman to receive the Nobel Peace Prize.

BIOMEDICAL SCIENTISTS

⇒ RACHEL SCHNEERSON ⇐
Born 1932

Rachel Schneerson is a cutting-edge scientist who is known for working with other awesome scientists to pioneer one of the most incredible medical breakthroughs of all time—a vaccine for a disease often known as Hib (*Haemophilus influenzae* type b). The deadly disease affected lots of children around the world, so Rachel worked with a team of scientists to develop a vaccine, which helped children develop antibodies against the disease. The vaccine has saved millions of lives across the globe. Rachel went on to work on other vaccines too. Her amazing discoveries have been used to help make other vaccines, which have saved even more lives!

ASTROPHYSICISTS

⇒ JEDIDAH ISLER ⇐
Born 1982

Jedidah is an awe-inspiring astrophysicist who checks out one of the coolest things in our universe—supermassive black holes. Black holes are found at the center of galaxies and gained their name because light cannot escape from them. Jedidah studies supermassive, hyperactive blackholes. These black holes are called blazars and have mega jets that fire out particles at a rate nearly as fast as the speed of light. Jedidah loved learning about space as a kid and she has worked with museums, libraries, schools, universities, and planetariums to inspire the next generation of scientists.

SIR DAVID ATTENBOROUGH
Born 1926

David is a legendary biologist, broadcaster, and writer who is fascinated by animals. As a child, he spent his days looking for bugs, amphibians, insects, and fossils. Since then, he's journeyed the world to teach us about the amazing lives of animals, from crocodiles and capybaras to polar bears and Komodo dragons. David has written, produced, appeared in, and narrated countless documentaries about why we must protect our planet. Lots of animals and plants are named after him, including a long-beaked echidna, a ghost shrimp, and a grasshopper. David even has an ancient reptile named after him—the Attenborosaurus! He tirelessly campaigns for ways in which we can battle against climate change.

UĞUR ŞAHIN AND ÖZLEM TÜRECI
Uğur born 1965 · Özlem born 1967

Uğur and Özlem helped to create a vaccine that saved lives around the world. When the global pandemic called COVID-19 arrived, it spread a new life-threatening disease across the entire planet, and so Uğur and Özlem's company, BioNTech, joined forces with a pharmaceutical company called Pfizer to create a lifesaving vaccine. Along with many other scientists, they worked incredibly fast to create a vaccine that would protect people against the virus, helping to save countless people from needing urgent hospital treatment. Uğur and Özlem have been married for more than twenty years.

NETA BAHCALL
Born 1942

Neta Bahcall is an astrophysicist and professor who wants to know whether the universe will keep expanding forever. Fascinated by the night sky and what lies beyond it, Neta maps out galaxies that are millions of lightyears across. She uses clusters of galaxies to trace bigger structures in the universe, pouring over images taken by amazing space telescopes. Neta learns about something called dark matter too, which is something in space that we can't see but that scientists know is there! Neta works with lots of other scientists and students to learn about our universe and is even figuring out how to weigh the universe.

⊰ FURTHER READING ⊱

Big Book of Bugs
By Yuval Zommer

Big Ideas That Changed the World:
Rocket to the Moon!
By Don Brown

Big Ideas That Changed the World:
Machines That Think!
By Don Brown

Big Ideas That Changed the World:
A Shot in the Arm!
By Don Brown

Buzzing with Questions: The
Inquisitive Mind of Charles
Henry Turner
By Janice N. Harrington

Fantastically Great Women Who
Changed the World
By Kate Pankhurst

Fantastically Great Women Who
Saved the Planet
By Kate Pankhurst

Finding the Speed of Light:
The 1676 Discovery That Dazzled
the World
By Mark Weston

How the Dinosaur Got to
the Museum
By Jessie Hartland

How the Meteorite Got to
the Museum
By Jessie Hartland

How the Weather Works: A
Hands-on Guide to Our
Changing Climate
By Christiane Dorion

Little People, Big Dreams:
David Attenborough
By Maria Isabel Sánchez Vegara

Little People, Big Dreams:
Mary Anning
By Maria Isabel Sánchez Vegara

National Geographic Readers:
Sharks!
By Anne Schreiber

The Questioneers: Rosie
Revere, Engineer
By Andrea Beaty

Science Comics: Dinosaurs:
Fossils and Feathers
By MK Reed

Science Comics: Sharks:
Nature's Perfect Hunter
By Joe Flood

Shark Lady: The True Story of
How Eugenie Clark Became the
Ocean's Most Fearless Scientist
By Jess Keating

Wangari Maathai: The Woman
Who Planted Millions of Trees
By Franck Prévot

Weather Words and What
They Mean
By Gail Gibbons

For Jakob, a little scientist
who inspires me ~S.G.

To Özgür, the rocket enthusiast
of my heart ~A.A.

The illustrations in this book were created in pencil and colored digitally.

Library of Congress Control Number 2022938969
ISBN 978-1-4197-6596-4

Text © 2022 Saskia Gwinn
Illustrations © 2022 Ana Albero
Cover © 2022 Magic Cat
Book design by Ella Tomkins and Maisy Ruffels

Printed and bound in China
10 9 8 7 6 5 4 3 2 1

Abrams Books are available at special discounts when purchased in quantity for premiums and promotions
as well as fundraising or educational use. Special editions can also be created to specification. For details, contact
specialsales@abramsbooks.com or the address below.

ABRAMS The Art of Books
195 Broadway, New York, NY 10007
abramsbooks.com